Not

How^ to Survive Quality Improvement

(A Primer for Quality Improvement Consultants, Senior Leadership, and Anybody Who Can Spell Q-U-A-L-I-T-Y)

Gregory Calloway

Copyright 2011 by
Gregory Calloway

QUALITY PLUS©

TXu 1-804-494 (Electronic Copyright Office)

ISBN - 13:978-0692827154
ISBN – 10:0692827153

CONTENTS

Dedication

This book is dedicated to the ladies in my life.

Beginning with my wife, Linda, who encouraged me to find an outlet for my frustrations. She understood the importance of having something in your life that you look forward to do. I know this journey that we've been on has not always been easy but I would not want to travel it with anyone else.

My daughter, Amber who showed the way. She was determined to reach her goals and she has worked tirelessly to accomplish them. In fact, she is the first in the family to get published. You are an inspiration to me. Not many fathers can say that.

Next, my daughter, Daralyn because she never fails to laugh. There is a saying that laughter is contagious. In her case, it is epidemic. Keep laughing and the world will laugh with you.

My mother, who has more faith than I can imagine. How many people can say that their mother is their role model. I know I am blessed.

My sister, Brenda who is steadfast and never gives up. I have to believe that good people are eventually rewarded.

My sister, Shirley, who has restored my faith that people can grow and reveal their true spirit.

All of these ladies have inspired me in one way or another.

Preface

Why I wrote this book

In the 1980's it became popular for corporations to bring in quality improvement consultants to improve their processes. Their motivation was to reduce costs, make their processes more efficient, or to increase revenue.

But First, a Fairy Tale

Once upon a time, in a land far, far away, there lived a king in a land known as Corporastan. Now this king, who was known as King Q, was a benevolent ruler. He was very satisfied with the quality of work of his citizens; however, he always had a feeling that things could be better. So he did what any ruler would do to improve his kingdom. He called Ye Olde Quality Consultants. These consultants were not just any consultants. They were the best quality improvement consultants in the land according to the Association of Professional Quality Consultants.

A wise and talented group were they. Some would even say that they're magical. These consultants had a reputation for improving kingdoms far and wide. Once they got their marching orders from the king, they met with his royal leadership team to ensure that the strategy and objectives of the kingdom were in alignment with that of King Q's vision. Being a wise group, they developed a Powerfully Pointed presentation to illustrate the current situation in Corporastan. These charts illustrated cascading goals and objectives and other non-existent terms of the time. Their next step was to meet with the middle-ages management team to ensure that they had read the mission and values statement of Corporastan.

After careful study and deliberation, the Ye Olde Quality Consultants determined that the king needed to hire them as consultants on a long-term basis with a pay as you go contract. Payment would be based on billable hours. The king agreed since he wanted to be taken seriously by his subjects as well as the kings from neighboring kingdoms.

The consultants first conducted an employee-satisfaction survey of the middle-ages managers. Results of the survey were not encouraging. They indicated that the citizens hated senior leadership and wanted to kill the king. Seeing that these results were inconclusive, the consultants suggested a teambuilding exercise.

The consultants determined that the best team building exercise was to have the team members go sailing at Lake Reindeer. This exercise would teach them to rely on each other. It would also show them that everyone has a role to play. After, this exercise, everyone would feel empowered. This was a location that the citizens had heard about but none could afford to attend. Lake Reindeer was usually off limits to all except those with lineage. Word was that this was the favorite location for senior leadership retreats. There were lakes and golf courses, lodges and cabins. It was also rumored that there were elves and gnomes at Lake Reindeer. Although, going to such a magical place was considered an honor, not everyone wanted to go. Hearing this, the consultants came up with a way to ensure that everyone would go and have a good time. Since this was a mandatory event, all citizens would have to attend. Therefore, the king first mandated that all citizens would have to sign an attendance sheet scroll (to prove that they were there) stating that they would attend the mandatory training so that they could become empowered to run their own operations.

Unfortunately, the day of the training was not the perfect day for sailing. It fact, what started out as a rainy day, soon developed into a storm. The freezing rain and frigid winds felt like mini daggers as they pierced the skin of the citizens. As should have been predicted, many citizens fell ill after sailing in the storm. Some even fell overboard. For the consultants, things could not have gone better.

Those who fell ill were immediately downsized. All others were notified that they would have to take a personality test so that they would know how they fit in the kingdom culture. The test asked such probing questions as what is your favorite magical spell, are you a knight or a jester, and what do you think of King Q.

After much deliberation, the consultants presented their findings to the royal senior leadership team. There was much anticipation throughout the land.

The results of the consultants' findings were presented at a mandatory all hands on board meeting.

What they found was truly astounding.

First, the kingdom needed to hire a permanent consulting company to monitor the continuous improvement in Corporaston. Second, all citizens would need to be downsized. The good news is that everyone could reapply for their jobs. The royal senior leadership team would all get bonuses for ensuring that this effort went smoothly.

The king was very pleased with these results. Of course, senior leadership was happy. And last but certainly not least, the citizens were happy. Those who kept their jobs were happy to have jobs. Additionally, they were presented with a chart that showed that the hierarchy of the organization had been turned upside down. The citizens were now at the top of the chart and the king was at the bottom (see the book cover). Unfortunately, this change did not include better pay. In fact, the citizens now had more work because they had to do the work of fellow citizens who were let go.

As for those who were let go, they all found similar jobs in other kingdoms that were also undergoing quality improvement initiatives.

Everyone lived happily ever after. The End.

Like you, I grew up hearing and reading fairy tales. They made my childhood a fun time. However, as I grew older, I realized that fairy tales are just that. I thought that I had left them behind when I reached adulthood. But now I wonder if I'm still hearing fairy tales.

I was drawn to the field of quality improvement after working for several years in the fields of accounting and finance for several large corporations. I was enticed by the prospect of making things better for myself and my co-workers. I thought, perhaps naively, that quality improvement would do magical things. It would empower employees, improve products and processes, and ultimately result in increased revenues for those businesses that improved their operations.

What I've learned subsequently, is that quality improvement means different things to different people. That like all products, it has to be sold and marketed. That perception is more important than reality.

I did not write this book to be cynical. Instead, I wanted to look at how absurd organizations can be at times. It is only through the lens of twenty-twenty hindsight that we can see how bizarre an insulated world can become when group-think takes hold. I'm not suggesting that people not join organizations. There are many rewards and benefits that can be had from working in an organization. There are also many pitfalls.

If you decide to play in this game, I hope you will find some tips in this book for surviving the experience. Additionally, I believe that we will get through life much better when we are able to laugh at ourselves and the odd situations that we sometimes find ourselves in. But mostly, we can laugh at those who have the arrogance to tell us that they are our leaders. Leadership is not a title. Instead, it is a role made possible only when there are individuals who willingly follow.

My experience working in the corporate world has taught me that fairy tales are just that. Furthermore, much of what we are indoctrinated with falls within the realm of fairy tales. More than any time in my life, I am realizing how important it is to think for oneself.

As a proponent of the field of Quality Improvement, it pains me to acknowledge that employees are often sold a bill of goods. Management may sometimes have ulterior motives that have nothing to do with improvement. There are lessons that I've learned from the many quality improvement initiatives that I've been involved in. For anyone who has been on a quality team, some of the lessons that I share in this book will be familiar. I hope that you find comfort in the fact that you are not alone.

For Quality Improvement Professionals, it is very important that you find a way to gauge the real culture in your corporate client's organization. If you accept management's version of the facts, you are doomed to failure. Make an effort to tap into the informal culture. Every organization has dual corporate cultures.

I wrote this book to show the pitfalls that can befall anyone in a corporate environment. Quality improvement is simply the vehicle that I chose to expose the duplicity of the "leaders" of a toxic environment.

One of the most important things I've learned is that when things are going badly in an organization, they usually don't get better. Move on. However, whether you move on or not, things always change.

Finally, I've learned that people are always going to be people...unpredictable. There is no process that can predict human behavior. Everyone looks out for themselves first regardless of what organization they work in. I've seen the biggest quality improvement cheerleaders turn from the mission as soon as the mission of the leader changed.

Fairy Tales are not real. Life is. Live life.

Acknowledgements

I would like to acknowledge all of the people I've worked with and for. I've learned something from everyone. I've learned a lot from the good leaders, but I've learned even more from the bad leaders. Learning what not to do is just as important as learning what to do. In fact, some of the best lessons come from these folks.

I would also like to thank all of the quality improvement professionals who dedicate themselves to improving the products, processes, and systems of companies around the world.

Gregory Calloway

Quality Plus© Consulting

Chapter 1 - Introduction to Quality

What is Quality? (Give me a Q, Give me a U, Oh Never Mind)

Words to Know
Product – Something that is made. Process – The act of doing something to produce a product or service. Voluntold – to be volunteered by your boss.

Quality is in the eye of the beholder. We all have different ideas about what quality is. OK, no one knows what quality is. But it is important. Not only is it important, it has to be improved.

How did the field of quality improvement get started. As best I can determine, some American guy (Deming) determined that things could be improved. Up until this point, this idea was unthinkable. He took his ideas to various business leaders in order to convince them that they could improve their profits by improving their products and processes. Whereupon, one executive asked, "what's a process?"

Since they were extremely successful and dominated their fields, they would not listen to this guru. Therefore, he took his ideas to the up and coming country of Japan. Since the Japanese were thought to have inferior products, they were willing to listen to him. He introduced his concepts to them, and they used them to make their products the best in the world.

That the concepts worked is undeniable. What is not certain is whether the success was due to the improvement of products or processes or both.

Product vs. Process

Product improvement is easy. It applies to automobiles, appliances and other tangible goods. It can be seen and felt. Process improvement on the other hand, is much harder to determine. What is a process? Where does it begin and where does it end? How does one document a process? These are all important questions for the quality improvement professional.

There is only one thing to do when you hear that your organization is about to undergo a quality improvement initiative. Duck and keep a low profile! Do not volunteer to lead any initiative or team. If the project fails, you will become the face of that failure. If you are "voluntold" to lead a team, quickly deputize the newest team member so that he or she will have to take responsibility should things not work out.

Chapter 2 - The Meeting: A Prelude

Words to Know
Journey - An imaginary trip that ends where it began.
Consultant - Someone who tells employees that what they are doing doesn't work. They usually suggest that their clients go on a journey.
Leadership Team - Hand-picked employees who are called leaders.

Global Telepathy Corporation (GTC), a fortune 500 company located in Atlanta had a reputation as a leader in its industry. It pays well and offers excellent benefits. An old line company, they were trying to stay up-to-date with the fast paced changes that most large businesses were under-going. One only had to look at the lobby walls to see that this was a conservative establishment. They were plastered with pictures of past Chief Executive Officers; all white haired white men. The ceilings were high and the floors were marble. Walking into corporate headquarters was like walking into a cathedral. The hugeness of the complex swallowed up all who walked its halls. Everything about the building was designed to tell people that they were insignificant.

Eric Diaz has worked at GTC as a financial analyst for approximately two years. He has worked for several companies in this capacity in the past. Eric is now at the age where he feels he has to make it (career-wise) or it will never happen for him. He has had several bad work experiences in the past but feels that GTC may finally be his big break. Eric graduated from college with average grades. He went to an average college and did not take his career or his future serious. As the first in his family to attend college, just graduating was an achievement in itself. Eric always wondered if the cold hard world of business was really for him. In fact, he was not sure what he wanted to accomplish in life.

Eric took pride in the fact that he always put his family first. His wife, Gloria was his chief career cheerleader. His little daughter, Natalie was the apple of his eye. Eric passed up several career opportunities to spend more time with his family. At the same time, he felt the pull to advance his career. It fact, he felt that it was either now or never.

At GTC, Eric believed that he finally found a place where he could build a career. GTC was known as a place that people didn't leave.

This all changed on a cool September Thursday morning. An email circulated throughout the department stating that there will be a "mandatory" meeting that afternoon. The GTC finance organization would be holding a meeting to discuss subjects that were "important to the life of the department." The office was all a buzz. What could this mysterious message portend for the department. Eric, being fairly new to the organization, asked some of his co-workers what this could mean. None of his co-workers had a clue about what to expect.

He noticed a group of employees huddled in the break-room. Eric approached the group to find out if anyone knew what this meant. No one seemed to know what to expect but there did not seem to be any panic. After all this is what large corporations do.

Eric returned to his cubicle with no more information than he left with.

The time arrived. Everyone assembled in the company auditorium. The buzz in the room was electric. Something was in the air. What would be this news that was "important to the life of the department." There was an air of excitement in the room.

On the stage sat the leaders of the department. Members of the leadership team chatted and seem unconcerned with the activity around them. Eric's supervisor, Frank Williams was among the members. Also, on stage was, Andrew Stone, the Executive Manager of the Global Acquisitions division. Andrew was a no nonsense guy. He could be charming in a calculated way. Clean-cut, Andrew was lean and mean. He said all the right things and apparently made all the right moves. If Andrew talked to you, you felt honored and afraid at the same time. Andrew was polished and clearly favored and trusted by the executive leaders. He was clearly a man on the move.

Although, Eric did not aspire to be like Andrew, he admired Andrew's dedication to advancing his career. Andrew wore tailor-made suits and spit shined shoes. His hair was dark and slicked back. He walked with purpose and focus. When he walked past you in the office, you could feel a faint breeze.

Also, on stage was Joseph Aldridge, Executive Vice President of Financial Management. He was the top officer of the division.

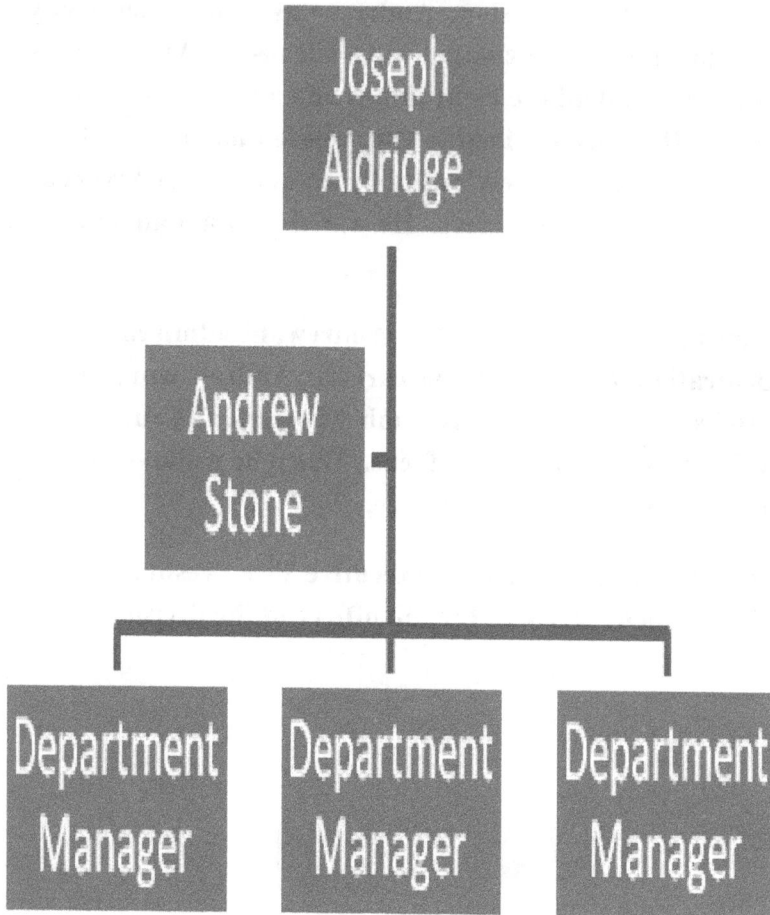

Global Telepathy Corporation: Finance Division

Mr. Aldridge would be invisible anywhere else. But here he was the supreme leader. Short in stature and slightly pudgy, Mr. Aldridge was seldom seen but when he was around, there was an air of importance. Mr. Aldridge or Elf as some of Eric's co-workers called him, wore suits right off the rack. He seemed to be someone who worked his way up to the top and never forgot or forgave the circumstances that caused him to struggle. He seldom smiled and when he did, it was a slightly sinister and mischievous smile. Without knowing why, Eric always felt uncomfortable around this man. Distance was a good thing.

Eric noticed that onstage with the Leadership Team were two people who were not familiar to him. This was obviously not a typical staff update. A well dressed young man and an even younger lady sat stage right and seemed to be huddled in preparation for their parts in this unfolding drama.

Although, the news to come was yet to be revealed, no one in the audience seemed to be concerned. In fact, everyone seemed relaxed. They were just happy to take a break from work and to gather socially out of the office.

Andrew Stone, who reported directly to Mr. Aldridge, called the meeting to order. He thanked everyone for taking time out of their busy schedules to take part in this important meeting. He then proceeded to tell what seemed to be around 70 to 80 people assembled why they were there.

"As you all know, we are in a very competitive business. We can no longer afford to be complacent." At this point, the auditorium had become completely quiet. Andrew continued, "In order to maintain our competitive edge, we will have to change. To tell you more about these changes, Mr. Aldridge will tell you why it is imperative why this change is needed. Joe?"

Mr. Aldridge rose from his seat slowly as if the act of standing was an imposition. He put his company issued brief case in his seat and sauntered to the podium. As he walked to the mic, he appeared to be checking his email messages on his smart phone. Everything about him indicated that there were more important things that demanded his attention. Although Mr. Aldridge was inconsequential in appearance, his presence demanded your attention. At this particular point, the audience was focused on him like a laser. Mr. Aldridge, cleared his throat and then, reluctantly looked up from his phone to address the department.

"Ladies and gentlemen, I don't have to tell you that we are in tough economic times. Our business is under assault like never before. I've asked my leadership team to look into ways that we could stay ahead of the competition. Based on our discussions, we looked to an outside firm to provide some guidance on what we need to do. Quality Plus© is a well-known quality improvement consulting firm. They will be meeting with you for the next several months to get your input on how we can be a better performing organization. Please give them your attention and cooperation." With that, he looked to a young well-dress man sitting to the side of the stage. "Jason, come up here and tell us what you've learned."

The well-dressed young man leapt to his feet and raced to the podium. "How are we doing this afternoon," he boomed. "Welcome to the 'Breakthrough Celebration' Meeting. As, Mr. Aldridge mentioned, we are Quality Plus. We have been in business for twenty years. We have worked with some of the most successful firms to help them to discover the strengths and opportunities for improvement." Eric couldn't help but hear "opportunities for improvement" as "weaknesses." He overheard someone behind him say "Here we go again."

What did this mean and why did the comment not seem in sync with the demeanor of the young man on stage. The speaker continued, "We have offices in over 30 countries. Over the next several months we will be working with you to identify ways in which GTC can be the best."

Jason Gunn, continued to take the department through a series of PowerPoint slides that illustrated that customer satisfaction was high but not as high as the benchmark figures that Quality Plus had gathered in their research.

Jason seemed to be unusually upbeat and energetic. The department heads, otherwise known as "The Leadership Team" sat attentive as they listened to the presentation. Although, it was not clear exactly what all this meant, several things stood out with Eric. Evidently, we would all be going through a journey and there would be a paradigm change. When Mr. Gunn mentioned that we would have the support of senior leadership, it was only then that Eric noticed that Mr. Aldridge had quietly left the stage. Although his seat was in the middle of the stage, no one seemed to notice when he departed. When Jason finished his presentation, he relinquished the stage to Andrew Stone.

"Any questions" asked Mr. Stone. There were none. "Ok, I won't hold you any longer. In the coming days, you will be learning more about this journey. Have a great afternoon".

As the meeting adjourned, the buzz returned to the hall. Everyone seemed to be happy that the meeting was over and since it was late in the afternoon; most people did not seem to be in a hurry to get back to work.

The next morning, Eric sensed a change in the office atmosphere. As he walked to his desk, he noticed that people were hard at work at their desks at a time when most people would normally be getting their first cup of coffee. As he walked to his desk, past the executive conference room, he noticed a new sign above the door which read "War Room." He also noticed that there were blank easel sheets all over the walls. If this wasn't mysterious enough, he saw two unfamiliar people huddled at the corner of the conference table. He was later to learn that this was Jason Gunn and Tanya Johnson from Quality Plus, a quality improvement consultant firm.

Chapter 3 - You've Been Picked to be on a Team. Now What?

Words to Know
Group think - brainwashing within an organization.
War Room - a conference room full of easels and charts. A room where employees talk strategy.
Brainstorming - Thinking of new ideas for solving problems without really thinking. Usually done in a War Room.

Before Eric could check his morning email messages, the telephone rang. Gladys, Andrew Stone's secretary was on the line. "Good morning, Mr. Diaz. I'm calling to inform you that Mr. Stone would like for you to come to a meeting in the Executive Conference Room at 9'O Clock." Knowing how much work lay waiting for his attention, Eric hoped that this meeting would not last long.

Eric grabbed a pad and pen and put on his jacket and then headed for the meeting. When he walked in, he saw Andrew Stone, Jason Gunn, and Tanya Johnson sitting at the head of the table. Also, in attendance, were some of his co-workers.

Shirley Anderson joined the company at about the same time as Eric. She was known to be friendly and easy-going. Eric had worked with her on earlier assignments and he valued her input. Shirley was respected for her professionalism. Eric had never heard a bad word about her.

Nick Anunzio, on the other hand, seemed to be unhappy with life in general. As one of the oldest members of the department, Nick had seen it all. He had managed to survive several changes in leadership as well as a never ending series of reorganizations. Eric sensed that Nick was not overjoyed to be at the meeting.

Frances Turner was new to the organization. Fresh out of college, she seemed to be too eager to please. Frances seemed overwhelmed but eager to learn.

Andrew stood up to announce that this meeting was the kick-off meeting for the self-directed work team environment envisioned by the department. Instead of a top down traditional hierarchy of managers leading subordinates, the department would now be organized into a cluster of teams that is composed of empowered employees who make their own decisions. Eric could not help but notice that Nick was not paying attention.

Next, Jason Gunn explained that this was the way most progressive companies were headed. The "team" was told that they would be reasonable for determining what the new team environment for the department would look like. They would conduct surveys and interviews with fellow employees to get their input on what this environment should look like. As Jason ran through yet another set of PowerPoint slides, Eric realized that Tanya Johnson never spoke.

As the meeting ended, everyone seemed to be excited about this new adventure. As Eric headed back to his desk, he notice several small groups of his co-workers huddled together in the recesses of the office. As he walked past them, several people nodded at Eric and then returned to whispered conversations.

Eric decided to head to the break-room for his second cup of coffee. There in the middle of a group of three or four fellow employees, was Nick. Not surprisingly, Nick was not excited about the "Journey" that the organization was about to embark on. "Here we go again," barked Nick. Eric recognized this voice as the skeptical voice from the staff meeting.

"How many times do we have to go through these changes." Nick held everyone's attention. "I've been here for 31 years. I've seen them come and go. Nothing ever changes. This is just another 'flavor of the month.' When Eric walked in, the group turned to him to gauge his reaction. "So Eric, you were in the meeting, what do you think?" asked one of the group members. "I'm willing to give it a chance" Eric said diplomatically. It was the right thing to say, but Eric had his doubts as well. He too had been through several quality improvement initiatives. The difference is, he had not stayed around long enough to see if any of them worked. Eric thought to himself, maybe Nick was right. Maybe he was getting caught up in group think. Even so, it is never good to openly express those views. Besides, maybe this time would be different. It had the support of Mr. Aldridge. Also, Andrew Stone was playing a direct role in the process. Surely, the organization would not devote so much time and effort to an initiative that it did not fully support. This was bolstered by the fact that word had spread that there had been several other teams meeting; each with their own focus.

Quality Plus Consulting set up a series of team meetings throughout the organization in order to build teams. Evidently, it takes more than sitting people in a room and calling them a team. Jason Gunn has notified Eric's team that there will be a team meeting to help accomplish this goal. And so a meeting was scheduled for Monday morning at 10am.

As he walked into the War Room, Eric noticed that there were easel sheets pasted on the walls of the room. These sheets had titles such as Mission Statement, Strategy, Team Name, and Team Leaders. As Jason explained it, this would be a long meeting with lots of ideas flowing from the teams on the easel sheets.

The first order of business was to choose a team name. Eric had given some thought to this and presented the team with the name "The A Team." Since no one else had a suggestion, this name was adopted by the team based on a voice vote. Next Jason suggested that the team would need a mission.

He handed each team member a pad of colored posted notes and scented markers. Each team member was to post at least 5 ideas on the wall. Frances began to write ideas immediately. In fact, before long, she asked for more Post It notes. Nick, on the other hand, leaned back in his chair and smelled each of his markers. "Um Strawberry." Nick was in no hurry to participate. After a few minutes, everyone began to write down ideas and then posted them on the sheets labeled "Mission Statement." After all ideas had been exhausted, Jason suggested that each member walk around the room and read the ideas that had been posted. Jason explained that the process of Brainstorming meant that ideas should come to us organically without much for-thought. Additionally, the rules dictated that team members not criticize other team members' ideas. As Eric walked around the board room, he read what other team members had written. "To be the vendor of choice for our customers, to provide the best service at the lowest cost in the most efficient manner." As the team members read the Post It notes, an air of accomplishment permeated the room. Next the team members were to vote on the Mission Statement that best represented their mission.

Next, the team was to select a Team Leader. Eric saw this opportunity as a way to get recognize by the Leadership Team. However, he did not want to seem to eager for the position. His concerns turned out to be unwarranted, as Frances nominated him for Team Leader. Nick seconded the nomination and it was a done deal. After one round of voting, it was official. Eric would be the Team Leader of the "Self-Directed Work Team Environment" Team (The A Team).

Next, the team was to develop a Work Plan. Frances immediately volunteered to type the plan. Before the day ended, the charts were full and the room actually resembled a war room. Jason congratulated the team on an excellent day of work. As the team members left the room, taking cookies and coffee with them, Jason took the sheets off the wall, rolled them into cylinders and then handed them to Tanya.

Based on the Team's Work Plan, the next order of business was Team Building. As Jason explained it, the team would have to attend training in order to determine how members could work together more effectively. The team would meet at an off-site location so that members would not be tempted to answer their telephones. Eric liked these meetings since he could dress casual. The only stipulation was that everyone would have to wear a polo shirt with the GTC logo on it.

As he walked into the ballroom of the downtown hotel, Eric surveyed the room to see where his team was sitting. He did not have to look far. In the middle of the ballroom sat a table with a sign on it reading "The A Team." As he looked around the room, he could see the names of the other teams; "The Champions, Team Q, The World Beaters. The odd thing about the groupings was that employees were no longer in their department groups but instead were now in their Quality Improvement Teams (QIT).

There was something oddly familiar about the setting. Was it the musty stale smell of the carpet, the dim lighting despite the oversized chandeliers, or the cold chill throughout the hall. Furthermore, this cavernous hall was much too big for the number of occupants.

Eric noticed that there was a long table in the back of the ballroom. On the table there were containers of coffee and plates of fruit and pastry. Eric immediately joined the line to get his morning java. Standing in front of Eric, was his Supervisor, Frank. "So Eric, how are things going with the A Team?" "I think we're making progress," chimed Eric. "What team are you on Frank?" Looking down as if in pain, he replied, "I'm on the Condors. We're having some problems. How about you guys?" Well, said Eric as he inched up in the line, "We seem to be having some personality conflicts. Frances is eager to start the improvement project as soon as possible even though other team members would like more time to plan. She said something about analysis by paralysis. Meanwhile, Nick wants to study everything to the nth degree before we do anything. I'm not sure what to do." Frank had a ready answer. "Ask Jason, that's what he's here for." Eric thought this was a good idea.

"Ok folks, let's get started," announced Eric. When Eric returned to his table, he noticed something that he had not seen before. Tanya was standing front and center. Grabbing the microphone, she glanced around the room. "Today, we will learn what makes teams effective. We will also learn about personality types and finally, we will learn how to deal with conflict." The last item was music to Eric's ears.

As Tanya spoke, Jason Gunn walked around the room handing out packets of colored paper at each table. "What you are now receiving are personality tests. Please fill them out as honestly as possible." The 70 or so employees took their number two pencils and studiously fill out the packets. As each person completed their packets, they were to write their personality types on the easel next to their table. Nick looked at Eric's comments and commented "I knew you were a feeler." Hearing this Eric immediately defended himself, "I think I'm more analytical." "No, you're definitely a feeler" Nick shot back. Not surprisingly, Nick's personality type was a cautious doubter. Frances was an optimistic extrovert. Eric thought this exercise to be interesting but not very useful. As the results were posted at each team's table, the crowd was full of excitement. As the teams moved to the adjoining ballroom for lunch, Nick yelled to Eric, "hey feeler, I'll try not to hurt your feelings." Although this was said in jest, Eric could not help but think that there was an underlying feeling of resentment associated with the comments. After all, Nick was the oldest member of the team. And although he did not want to be voted as Team Leader, he made it obvious to the rest of the team that he had more experience and knowledge than anyone else.

After lunch, Andrew Stone joined the meeting. His first comment was "Thank you for taking the time out of your busy schedules to attend this very important training." "Not that we had a choice" whispered Nick. "Yeah, the email notice said the meeting was mandatory" chimed another voice at the table. Not wishing to be left out, Eric commented, "Yeah, I guess this was important to the life of the department." Although, Eric could not commit himself to this mutiny, he was bothered by the fact that there was a sign-in sheet for these "trusted" employees.

Andrew continued, "As Mr. Aldridge says, employees are our most important assets. You are all doing great work and I wanted to take this time to acknowledge this fact. The future is uncertain as we travel on this journey, but you all should know that even though the organization may look different at the end of the process, no one should be afraid that they will lose their jobs." This last comment raised a red flag for Eric since the possibility of job lost was not in his conscience thought - until now. Eric looked toward Nick. Nick looked back at Eric and nodded. The thought entered Eric's mind, what if Nick is right?

Next Andrew dropped a bombshell. "Although we are pleased with the progress the teams have made, we will be reducing our reliance on Quality Plus." What did this mean? One thing was certain, Andrew was not about to tell them any more than he wanted them to know.

Lessons Learned
Don't Commit to Any New Projects
Don't Volunteer for Any New Projects
Look to See Who's in the Game – Who is Actively Supporting the Initiative, Who is Laying Back
Don't Ignore the Reactions of the Long-Time Employees – They Survived for a Reason
Pay Attention to All Meetings – Formal (e.g., Corporate Auditorium) and Informal (e.g., Coffee Break Room)

Chapter 4 - Don't Tease Me Bro

The next meeting of the "A Team" was very interesting. For the first time, Tanya was not present at the meeting. As Jason explained, she was reassigned to another client. Jason seemed to be deflated as was true of the team members. Things are changing and communication did not seem to be as free flowing as previously.

Eric noticed that Andrew was not as visible as he had been in the past. In fact, his door was closed more often than in the past. Jason explained to the team that he would not be present at all of the meetings going-forward. However, he would provide the training material (PowerPoint Slides) to the team.

The first day of training without Quality Plus was a study of the history of Quality.

As the defacto team trainer, Eric made a conscious decision to avoid certain words and phrases that Jason was fond of using. No longer would the team be admonished to think outside of the box or to change their paradigm.

Eric starts the Power Point presentation. The first slide is entitled "The GURUS."

Each slide tells a little about the pioneers of Quality Improvement:

Joseph M. Juran – The Human Side of Quality, Pareto Principle or 80/20 Rule, Fitness for Use

W. Edwards Deming – Made trips to Japan to help them improve their product quality, introduced 14 Points of Management, which, he said, have one aim; to make it possible to work with joy.

Philip B. Crosby – Quality Management Concept of Zero Defects (ZD)

Walter A. Shewhart – Statistical Quality Control, Shewhart Cycle

Armand V. Feigenbaum – TQM

Kaoru Ishikawa – Fishbone or Cause and Effect, Concept Focus on the Customer

After lunch, the team reviewed slides that addressed the Quality Process.

One slide in particular caught Shirley Anderson's attention. It says, "Each process has customers with inputs and outputs." "Who are our customers?" asked Shirley. Eric volunteered, "Our customers are the internal clients that we provide financial reports to." "No", responded Nick, "I think our customers are the Leadership Team. They're the ones that we have to please."

After several hours of PowerPoint Slides, Eric came to the realization that even the consultants were now suffering from "Chart-Itis." Having exhausted all possible solutions for the topic of the day, Eric called the meeting to a close.

Chapter 5 - You're Empowered. Now Do As I Say!

(Insurrection in the Break Room)

Words to Know
Flavor of the Month – Another failed project that will last until another project is identified. A new quality improvement initiative. If you survive one of these, have no fear, another one will come along very soon. Even if one initiative appears to be successful, new management will want to introduce their own initiative. If fact, if you are around long enough, you will see some of the same projects come around again. In some cases, the names have changed. R.I.P. – Retired in Place Old Head – Old Employee

On Monday morning Eric noticed a small group of co-workers were having a meeting in the Break-room. Though they were speaking in hushed tones, the pantomime of their gestures made it clear that the discussion was intense. As Eric approaches the room, he notices that no one notices him. In the center of a circle of co-workers was Nick. "This is just another Flavor of the Month," Nick exhorts his co-workers. "I've seen these guys come and go. Just watch. Andrew will probably be gone before long." Not wanting to be discouraged, Eric goes back to his desk to check his email messages. His mind can't move on from Nick's comments. He wondered, "Could it be true?"

Unable to concentrate on work, Eric decides to seek out one of the other Old Heads. Eric walks down to Kenneth Walker's desk. Kenneth was a typical Old Head. He wore hush puppies and khaki pants and a sweater on most days. "Hi Kenneth, how is your team doing?" Seeming unwilling to commit to an answer, Kenneth replied, "It's going OK." Eric persisted. "Do you think this quality improvement initiative is going to work?" Kenneth simply shrugged his shoulders. Sensing that he would get no response from Kenneth, Eric moved on.

As he walked back to his desk, Eric bumped into Frances. Before Eric could say anything, Frances spoke up. "I saw you talking to Kenneth. I wouldn't waste my time talking to him." Eric's curiosity was aroused. Turning to her he asked, "Why do you say that Frances?" Then Frances said something that he had never heard before. "He's R.I.P." "R.I.P.?" Eric repeated. Frances explained that R.I.P. stood for "Retired in Place." "He is just trying to put his time in so that he can retire in 4 years." Eric recognized this malady. It was general knowledge that these are employees who have been around forever. At some point, they've made the decision to do as little work as possible without getting fired. Their chief motivation is to hang in there until retirement. The last thing the Old Heads wanted was to rock the boat.

Based on his conversation with his co-workers, Eric realized that there are informal teams in the organization. He also realized that, at some point, he might have to choose sides. What would it be; Coffee Party or Tea Party, Bloods or Crips?" When he first arrived in the organization, Eric pledged to himself that he would not ever wear anyone's gang colors. Now there was the prospect of being put in a position where he would have to choose. He remembered one thing Kenneth had said. "Why don't you talk to Andrew? He used to be one of us. He started as a middle manager." To Eric, the idea of Andrew being one of us or coming from us was unfathomable. This got him to thinking, 'Do people change once they reach a certain level or was he always who he is and that's what propelled him to his current position.' Nonetheless, Eric decided to follow Kenneth's suggestion.

Lessons Learned
Trust No one
Follow the 80/20 Rule – 80% of the People You meet will be A-Holes, but it's still worth it to get to know the 20% who are not

Chapter 6 - Selling the Plan

Words to Know
LINO© – Leaders in Name Only
The fact that someone is on the leadership team does not automatically make that person a leader. To be a leader, someone has to want to follow you.

Eric contacted Gladys and requested a meeting with Andrew. Although he had been in Andrew's office before, he could not help but be impressed with the expansive desk; dark brown and made of real oak, the globe sitting on the conference table, the cabinet containing the closed-circuit TV and of course the wall map full of push pins indicating the global locations of GTC. "What can I do for you Eric?" Andrew asked. "Well, Andrew, I happened to notice that the number of staff meetings have decreased since the beginning of the project." Sensing Eric's unease, Andrew interrupted, "not to worry. Everything is on track. I want to commend you on the job you and your team are doing. I want you to know that you guys are empowered to do whatever you think is best for the organization. Please let me know what I can do to support you guys." With that, Andrew stretched his arm out to shake Eric's hand. At once, Eric realized that he had been dismissed.

Because of his unique position as a Team Leader, Eric had access to Senior Leadership. But as time went by, he learned that some of those who were called leaders were not leaders at all. There was a formal culture; the organization, and an informal culture; the Break Room. Also, he determined that he could get more useful information from the "real leaders" like Nick rather than the designated leaders. In fact, these leaders were actually LINOs©; Leaders in Name Only.

Lessons Learned
Watch out for LINOs© - Leaders in Name Only
Pay attention to who's selling the plan

Chapter 7 - You Are Not In Compliance (Switching Gears)

Words to Know
QHMP© - Quality Help Me Plan

The email hit Eric's desk like a thud. Andrew Stone had agreed to a promotion to Executive Vice President of the Mergers and Acquisitions group. Beginning May 10th he could be reached at his new office at corporate headquarters.

What did this mean for the Quality Improvement initiative? Several emotions took over. The overwhelming feeling was one of betrayal. Before he could head to the Break Room to get the latest take on the news, Nick was at his desk. "What did I tell you? Do you really think a star player like Andrew would leave if he thought this was gonna be a successful project?" 'Good Point,' thought Eric. Eric began to wonder if he could believe anything from senior leadership. Nick continued, "There is only one thing that matters to each of us." Eric wondered what that one thing could be. Nick explained that it was radio station WIIFM (What's In It For Me). Eric realized that Andrew was only looking out for himself all along. Game, Set, Match! Nick was more than a little pleased to be proven right. Eric now realized that he might need his own quality plan. He needed his own quality plan to survive the Quality Plan. He needed a QHMP (Quality Help Me Plan).

Lessons Learned
WIIFM (What's In It For Me) May be found on either the AM or FM dial.

Chapter 8 - Congratulations on Achieving Breakthrough Results – You're Fired!!!!

Words to Know
ABR – Achieving Breakthrough Results©
QUIT© - Quality Under Institutional Tyrant

The date was set for each team to roll out their Breakthrough Quality Improvement Initiative. Each team leader was to present their recommendations to the entire organization. Eric was nervous but confident. He had rehearsed the presentation numerous times. His main concern was not the material, but rather would it be convincing. Eric had lost complete faith in senior leadership.

There was an air of excitement in the auditorium. In addition to the team leaders, Mr. Aldridge was on the stage. He even seemed to pull himself away from his Blackberry long enough to pay attention. Also, on stage were the two consultants from Quality Plus©. This was a major production. There was music and balloons. Each employee was handed a pair of sunglasses as they entered the room. The glasses were emblazoned with the GTC logo. There were door prizes, food and drinks.

As each team leader completed their presentation, the audience erupted into applause. At the end of the presentations, Mr. Aldridge leapt to the podium. "Please join me in congratulating the teams on a great job. I believe this plan will result in breakthrough results. Thank you for your diligent work on this project. The Leadership Team will let you know about the next steps for Phase II of this ABR project." These words sounded strange to Eric since the Leadership Team had not lead on this project. Nick's words repeated in Eric's mind, "watch who's selling the plan." Judging from the puzzled looks around the room, Eric was not the only one confused. All of the air had been sucked out of the room.

The following week, members of the Leadership Team called separate meetings of their teams. This seemed like the old hierarchy to Eric. Frank Johnson summoned Eric to his office and told him to call a meeting of his team.

Once in the War Room, Frank dropped a bomb on the self-directed work team. A week from today, everyone in the organization will meet in the auditorium to take a test. According to Frank, the purpose of the test was to determine compatibility of team members. As the meeting closed, Frank asked if there were any questions. There were none. The members of the team walked out of the room as if they were in a funeral procession.

Test Day – A Friday

On the following Friday, all employees were to gather in the company auditorium. Everyone was to sign in with their department's administrative assistant prior to finding a seat. The atmosphere was now completely opposite of the Breakthrough Celebration Day. No music, no food, no drinks, no door prizes. Only number 2 pencils and a test booklet. It wasn't long before Eric realized that this was a different kind of test. Some of the questions were from the list below:

Choose your favorite flower
What is your favorite color car?
Choose the emotion that you most identify with

And so it went. As each employee completed their test, they handed in their number 2 pencil and their test booklet. As he walked out, having no idea how he did on the test, the administrative assistant repeated the same line to everyone. "Have a nice weekend."

The following Monday morning, the office was a completely different environment that the one the employees left on Friday. There were employees gathered in small groups and talking in hushed tones. There was Frances, and Nick and the others. Those who were not standing in a group were at their desk. Eric noticed that these folks were putting their belongings in boxes. Only one word came to mind – surreal. Frances pulled Eric to the side and told him to check his email right away. There was a message from Mr. Aldridge. You are to come to the War Room at 8:45am – 15 minutes from now. By now, Eric could literally hear his heart beating. Boom, boom, boom, the sound growing louder with each heartbeat.

At 8:40, Eric steeled himself and began the march to the War Room. This time that name seemed to have a different meaning.

As he entered the room, there on one side of the table was a solitary chair. On the other side sat Mr. Aldridge, Andrew Stone and a gentleman unfamiliar to Eric. Mr. Aldridge, whose quality philosophy was often derided by the staff as Q.U.I.T. (Quality Under Institutional Tyrant), introduced the stranger. "Eric, this is Hugh Scott. He is from our legal department. Based on the results of the test last week, it has been determined that you are not compatible with the new mission of GTC." The words landed with a thud. Now in a daze, Eric struggled to comprehend what was said from this point forward. One thing seemed certain, there were no options. Mr. Scott took over the conversation. "Eric, I'm sure that your skills will take you far." Eric finished the thought in his mind…"Just not here." Your employment with GTC is being terminated. You will be re-assigned to our call center for the next six months. Mr. Scott slid a large brown envelop across the desk towards Eric. "Please do not share this information with anyone. Please review this confidentiality agreement. If you agree with the terms, you will receive a lump sum payment. Do you have any questions?" Eric had a question, but it was a question for himself. 'How do you maintain your dignity and composure in the face of a full-on frontal attack?' Eric left the room feeling numb. After all he had been one of the leaders of the quality improvement initiative. Other people came to him to find out the status of the project. How could he have been so blind? As he walked to his desk, his co-workers looked away. As he passed Frank, he extended his hand to shake his hand. Frank pulled his hand back as if to indicate that a simple handshake with Eric was contagious. Eric heard himself saying, "Don't worry, I'm OK." When he reached his desk, all Eric could think of is 'it's over.' At once, a feeling of sadness mixed with relief overcame him.

As he was packing his things, Nick came to his desk and shook his hand. "It's the 80/20 rule", Nick exclaimed. Eric knew the 80/20 rule from his quality training but he had no idea why it applied in this situation. Nick explained, "80 percent of the people you meet will be A-Holes but it's well worth it to get to know the 20 percent who are not." Eric understood and he thanked Nick for his compassion. Nick was saved from the downsizing.

What lessons could be learned from this experience? What are the next steps? How does one regain his pride?

Eric and seven of his colleagues were let go. All based on a test that made no sense to any of them. Eventually, everyone landed on their feet to battle yet more quality improvement initiatives at their new employers. Eric learned some valuable lessons from his experiences at GTC. The fairy tale has been fractured and now he was free to live in the real world. Through it all, Gloria, his wife, stood by him and supported him without reservation.

Some Final Thoughts

Trying to understand why leaders make the decisions that they make is useless. Don't dwell on it. It is a complete waste of time. Instead, put yourself and your family first. Always have a back-up plan (a Plan B), no matter what. Remember, things always change.

As a member of the baby boom generation, I bought into the fairy tales. Go to college, get an education and you will get a good job and a rewarding career. Stay loyal to the company and they will be loyal to you. If you play by the rules, you will be rewarded.

Although these things are possible, for many of us they were never realized.

So, where does that leave us? First of all, our kids will learn from our experiences. They won't make the same mistakes. Secondly, there is always hope. Take control over your own life. Your life belongs to you. Do what brings you joy and never let someone else dictate your work life.

I wish you your best life. In the end, the choice is yours.

Gregory Calloway

About the Author

I am the chief Continual Improvement Consultant (CIC) at Quality Plus©, a quality improvement consulting firm.

I was born in Newark, New Jersey and I still consider it home. However, the world is much too big to limit yourself, and therefore, I am also a citizen of the world.

This book is a culmination of the many adventures that I experienced after beginning my professional career as an accountant. After several false starts with small companies, I began a rewarding career with a Fortune 500 company. There, I had many careers....accountant, financial analyst, and internal auditor. The most rewarding experience was the one that introduced me to the field of quality improvement. I think it tapped into my latent desire to make things better.

At this company, I was fortunate to be a member of several quality improvement teams that worked on and received a company-wide quality award, which was based on the National Malcolm Baldrige criteria.

My credentials in the field of quality improvement include being certified as a Manager of Quality/Organizational Excellence (CMQ/OE) by the American Society for Quality. Additionally, I am a member of the Institute of Internal Auditors. Most of my professional experience as been in the fields of accounting and finance.

Recently, I realized another long-held and latent desire. I became a teacher, an accounting instructor to be more exact. Experiencing "leadership" in different environments is what led me to where I am now. I've determined that it is the quality of the leaders that makes all the difference in the world. Now, my eyes are wide-open.

All of these experiences, good and not so good, have led me to another latent desire. I have written this, my first book.

Thank you for taking this journey with me. The journey continues.

Greg

gregcal50@gmail.com

Quality Plus©
"Taking Your Business to the Next Level"